Nobody F***ing Told Me:
"Mess"ays from Motherhood

by Sammie Prescott

Eliezer Tristan Publishing
Portland, OR

Cover design by Aaron J Smith

For my D.I.L.F of a husband who has loved me through every wild idea, mental breakdown and curveball. Thanks for laughing at my jokes and giving me two wild boys. Can't wait to hunt Bigfoot with you when this book allows us to retire.

Special thanks to my Girls, who've helped shape me and this book. I wouldn't be nearly as funny as I am (or as I think I am) if it weren't for you guys being the best hype women on planet earth.

Table of Contents

Introduction: What is a "Messay?"

WRITING A BOOK is really hard, especially when it's about your real life. I could write fiction forever. It's what I always wanted to do. But here I am, sitting at my secondhand kitchen table writing about my life as a Mom, wife, and self-identified basket case. My name is S, and I have two beautiful boys and a hot husband. My oldest son is Tater, and my littlest is Tot. I refer to my husband as Sasquatch or 'Squatch, both in this book, and in real life.

I'm not anyone famous, nor am I as funny as I think I am. I'm just a regular person in dirty yoga pants with a really bad sense of humor. When I decided to write this, it wasn't because I wanted it to be a bestseller or for it to make me insane amounts of money. It wasn't so it would turn into a movie where Amy Poehler plays me. Really, it was for me. Everything I wrote started as a way to make me sane again, like an act of self-care. I was knee-deep in postpartum depression when I started this venture. It took another baby and a trip around the mental illness sun to get this bad boy published.

Here I am writing this book for you, for me, for really anyone who will take the time to read it. There is one problem though... No one has time to read books. That's why there are 40,000 "mom blogs." It's hard picking up a book to read four paragraphs before someone interrupts you, and then wondering what the hell just happened. Six days later when you pick the book back up, you literally have no clue what you just read about. I've been there, and it kind of sucks. Before kids, I was able to read a book in two days. Now I've been working on the same guide to inner peace for like two years.

So instead of grabbing a book, we reach for our phones and we read a blog about some Mom's perfect, Pinterest-worthy chicken dinner. I see their perfectly curled hair and vacuumed car. I know who I am and who my people are... and we just aren't those Moms.

These are all short stories from my world. Everything you're about to read has really happened. This is the book for people who don't have time to read one giant story or self-help book. This is a book that you can read while pooping or hiding in the bathroom pretending to poop (don't even say you've never done that. EVERYONE does it). This is the book for the school pick up line, since you're stuck in the same spot because no one will move forward. I'm talking to you, grey minivan...

I'm not going to tell you how to clean your house for inner peace, or how to brown butter for squash soup. I'm here to be real with you all. Whether you are a new parent or a seasoned veteran with 10 kids, I'm here. I'm here to teach you, laugh with you, and probably cry too. I cry a lot, and most of you do too. It's just a Mom thing.

This is a look into my life, and there is a really good chance it's a look into yours too. Because this is literally a look into the life I lead, you are going to hear it exactly how it happened. Curse words and all. My sense of humor is crass, and sometimes really fucked up. Maybe you should turn this into a drinking game: Drink whenever this lady drops an "F" bomb.

I prefer to call this a collection of Messays, if you will. When it boils down to it, my life is a mess. A beautiful, sticky, sappy, emotional, frustrating mess. For the longest time, I wanted to be the perfect Mom with the clean car and the perfect curls. After a lot of breakdowns and failed MILF diets, I've accepted that I'm just a Mom, who's kind of a hot mess, usually with a little mascara on my eyelid. So please, enjoy my "mess"ays, the really bad poems, and the notes. They're all true and from my soul.

Little thoughts

Kids are basically little fuckin' fruit-
snack dumpsters.

Pre-Mom Talents

"I have two brains in my body, but I've never felt so dumb." - Sofia Vergara, *Modern Family*

I WAS DRIVING along the highway while pregnant. It was snowing, because I live in the freaking tundra. I had a pumpkin spice latte in my cup holder, and I was jamming out to some Taylor Swift. Did I mention I was in a Volkswagen Bug? No? Well I was, and it was adorable.

A little back story, pregnancy was not prime nor was it even fun. There was no glow, just sweat. I wasn't in tune with my body or mind... Really, I was just a ragging bitch with a lot of back acne. I was consistently sick, sore, and hormonal.

I was a freaking DREAM. How my husband dealt with me is so far beyond my knowledge. Had he started crying and throwing up while wetting himself, I probably would have left. He is truly a better person than I am.

I was driving. We were doing 30 MPH on a major highway because no one knows how to drive in the snow. I mean, come on! I was in a BUG, a two-wheel drive plastic Barbie car, and I could still drive successfully in the snow. I could see about a car length in front of me, and we just crawled past the city. When traffic finally started moving, I began to feel sick.

This happened all the time, and I thought I knew what to do. I took long deep breaths and started counting to 10.
1….2….3…..4……..4……….4….
Fuck.

I was going to throw up. I felt the fiery lava building in my gut. I had about 4 seconds before everything I ate in the last 2 hours came up for revenge exorcist style (I had eaten a lot...). With some quick thinking and redneck engineering, I poured my latte out the window in 22 degree weather and placed the topless cup into my cleavage. My boobs were the perfect cup holder. They hugged that paper cup like it was their job.

Without taking my eyes off the road, I threw up into my cleavage cup. Tears rolled down my face as lava poured from my insides. I felt the burn of all-day sickness in my nose and my heart.

Within seconds, it was over and I felt fine. Even though I just threw up while driving, I felt like I had just won the Olympics. I threw up while driving, and no one died.

I put my vomit cup in the cup holder, put the lid back on it, and proceeded to where I was going. It was almost like nothing had happened. No one would ever know, had I not told them.

It was small victories that made pregnancy worth it. I mean, not that throwing up in a cup is cool or cute or anything. Because really, it's freaking gross - but I did not puke on myself. It was one of those moments that no one else cares about, but you still feel like pregnancy wobbling around a child-sized track to 'We Are the Champions.'

I got to where I was going and looked at my door. There was a giant frozen streak of orange on my car. It wasn't vomit though, so who really cares.

Little thoughts

The people who write the jingles for children's television shows are mouth breathers.

Play Dating

DATING ALWAYS totally sucked. You have to find someone who shares mutual interests and beliefs with you. Someone who you are comfortable with, and just generally enjoy the presence of this other human being.

I thought this whole "seeking someone" thing was over when I got married to the man my dreams... But it turns out that finding "Play Dates" is a lot like dating... There needs to be a Mom Tinder.

There is so much thought that goes into this whole "play date" process when you've never met this person before. You wonder what the Mom will be like, and how you'll interact with her. What if they don't vaccinate?!

And what about the kid... What if the baby is a total jerk? What if my kid is a total jerk? Do I smell weird? What if I get forehead sweat?! What if I have to poop?

Yeah, all of that ran through my head while I was driving the 2.6 miles to my very first, almost-blind playdate. Luckily, I had been talking to this Mom since September of 2014. The crazy thing is we belong to the same birth board on BabyCenter. We commented on mutual posts. A few months ago, there was a post about finding a Mom friend. Basically, people were sharing the cities they lived in to try and make connections with local people.

I know... Not the safest idea, but what the hell. We were both in the same city! We messaged one another for a few days and then moved our conversation over to Instagram. We had discussed getting together, but between holidays, sicknesses and just downright busy lives, we kept putting it off. This was the week we FINALLY scheduled a time to get not only our kids together, but us too. I read her blog, so I already knew we had mutual interests, but that still didn't change the fact that I was nervous.

I told 'Squatch and he so kindly pointed out the fact that this lady could totally be a serial killer. I rolled my eyes and said, "She seems totally normal."

His response then was, "I bet that lady who stabbed that pregnant woman from Craigslist seemed normal too."

REALLY?! That totally made my anxiety better... NOT.

But regardless of my nervous diarrhea and anxiety, I got into my car and headed over there. My hands were clammy as I turned my steering wheel into her driveway. "I can do this," I muttered to myself. I got Tater out of the car and saw her standing in the doorway. I was as nervous as a 15-year-old boy picking up his first homecoming date.

Then it happened. I came inside and there was no chainsaw or weird torture device. There was no crazy mural of Nicolas Cage on the walls. In fact, the house was beautiful and smelled like

Christmas. We brought the babies into the living room and hit it off. We talked, laughed, and I generally enjoyed her company. I did it! I survived my first play date!

I never knew going on a playdate would work someone up so much. Who knew that "Mom Dating" was totally a thing.

With my first "blind play date" out of the way, I totally feel more confident with doing it again.

Little thoughts

Maybe my toddler isn't sticky at all.
Maybe I'm just a weird, dry lizard
person.

Modern Motherhood

MODERN MOTHERHOOD is the weirdest, deepest connection. There is a chance that if you have procreated and have social media that you are in some sort of Facebook "Mom group." Between schedules that couldn't be any busier and social anxiety being at an all-time high, Mom groups seem to be the most efficient way for us to get adult interaction. These groups range from intimate groups of local friends to thousands of women spread all the way across the world.

For a long time, I avoided the Mom group scene because I thought I was way too cool for that. Reality hit me when I was 2 years in and only had like 2 friends, neither of whom had kids. A mutual friend started the group, and I didn't leave immediately like I do with most. At first, I could have given two shits about the group. I never posted, because again - too cool. A few months in, a topic came up that I was interested in and chimed in. Not to toot my own horn, but I'm like really funny (and modest). I started connecting with some of the ladies and making them laugh. I love to make people laugh. I butt heads with a few, but overall, I had found people that lifted me up, even the ones that make me fucking crazy.

I used that positive experience to join a few more. That's when the cold hard reality of the internet educated me. I learned something, and I learned it fast.

There are only two types of these groups…

A) A slightly less psychotic group of women, who talk shit behind each other's backs.
B) Balls to the wall smack down of Moms.

You might be thinking "Well that just can't be true!" Well it can be, and it is.

'Group A' begins mellow and stays mellow for the most part. There is an occasional drama post or ass chewing, but for the most part, it stays pretty respectable. People become friends, eventually meet in person. Then you start learning who people really are. The ones who you thought were the perfect humans reveal their true colors and intentions. It's not always bad, but it's not always good either. When it's bad, it leads to a friendship heartbreak. Losing friends, even when they turn out to be bad people, hurts. It's amazing how attached we get to other Moms.

In 'Group B,' one minute you're having a conversation about buying a pressure cooker and the next, it's a total blood bath. Passive aggressive statements and fact links begin to fly before you can even wrap your head around what just happened. The name calling begins, and then the private side messages start. God forbid you post a photo of your kid with a slightly Basque chest clip... These women – these strangers - are absolutely ruthless. They will tear you up and spit you out unless you know how to play the game.

You make your own little circle of friends within these groups, messaging each other back and forth. The alliances form like cliques in a cafeteria. You can't stop watching the drama even though you "hate" drama. Let's be honest, we may hate being a part of drama, but we sure do like sitting on the sidelines watching. Facebook Mom groups are like a terrible car accident that you can't stop watching.

I think these groups could be so valuable if we could all just treat each other right and realize that sometimes text and tone aren't transparent. When we choose to really show who we are on social media, it's vulnerable. It's so easy to pretend to be someone else. I see it all the time. Not everyone will get along, because that's just life. However, if we are open minded and honest about who we are, these groups would be such a beautiful thing.

Little thoughts

Little kid undergarments are way too expensive to constantly have shit stains on them.

Sick Babies

"Toddlers are germ warfare machines in a cute package." – Debora Geary

[1]**I'M LYING IN MY BED** at 8:06 am on a Friday. Normally this would be an amazing morning! My child is still asleep and the husband is at work. It's like the book, "T'was the Night Before Christmas." No one is saying shit and it's so peaceful. Hell, the neighbor's dog isn't even making its morning appearance.

This morning has sucked. My little bundle of love was up from 10 pm last night until 6 am. We've had a sick household the past 3 nights. It started with one night of vomiting, the second night of soul-shattering diarrhea, and

---

[1] This is not a story to read while eating, or for the faint of heart. This shit is real and contains a lot of shit. LITERALLY. You have been warned.

then last night of both fever and wanting to play. Having a sick toddler is like a really passionate yoga class (not that I do a ton of yoga, because who the fuck has time for that). It's a mind, body[2] and soul experience.

The sickness always seems to hit them in the middle of the night. I can handle vomit literally any other time but 3 am. It's also nature's law that they get stomach bugs on the nights where you have something for dinner that you really don't want to see a second time. This specific sickness, we had chili mac. I'll let you enjoy that visual for yourselves.

Literally, exactly around 3 am, I hear the tears and then the gag. The 'Squatch and I roll out of bed. Well, I roll... he leaps like a god damn spring chicken. We walk into what seems like an eruption of my own personal hell. I start

---

[2] By "body," I mean bodily fluids. Close enough, right?

the bath while he gets the kid naked. It just keeps coming. I can hear every lingering sound effect from down the hall.

This is where the mind experience comes in. As you listen to your child gagging, you have to find a center in your mind so that you also don't vomit. The whole time, all I thought of was a *Wheel of Fortune* episode that I watched with my dad when I was 16. It's funny how we remember these things at the most convenient times.

With team work and a few tears, we got the kid in the bath so that whatever eruption was coming next would be a contained blast. I went to his room where his newly-acquired Paw Patrol sheets were filled with a present I didn't want. This is where the body* experience come in. There is a lot going on, and at 3 am, I'm not the person to handle this. I start gathering the bedding and manage to get as little bodily fluids as I can on me. The larger regions of nastiness managed their way into a plastic bag. I got the sheets, blankets and stuffed animals into the washing machine, which for some reason is down stairs... When did laundry shoots go out of style?

(Just a side: HOUSING DEVELOPERS PUT THE DAMN LAUNDRY CLOSET WITH THE BEDROOMS!)

Everything is in the washer and I can hear water splashing. At least this child is somewhat happy while the liquid Voldemort is flying out of his body. This is where the soul comes in. I sit on the stairs and start praying to every single God that I can think of, which is a surprising amount considering it's 3 in the morning. I beg the power of the universe that this is a one-time event and that this little human will go back to sleep, in his own bed, and be happy as a damn clam after 7 am. I bargain with these prayers. I swear I'll clean my house more often and I apologize for the one time I didn't pick up dog poop at the park 8 months ago. You really put your whole soul into the hope of sleeping again.

After I stopped crying, I replaced his sheets – and by sheets, I mean I covered his bed in towels because why would I be prepared for an event like this? I get fresh pajamas and prepare for the arrival of the small person.

"Please be a fluke, please be a fluke," I keep whispering. I go back to the praying and wait.

We get him dry and clothed. We try to tuck him in when the water works start. When you are a parent of a toddler, you really need to pick your battles because no one is equipped for a 3 am temper tantrum. Against my own personal wishes, he comes to bed with us. I don't like co-sleeping. I know, I'm SUCH a bad Mom. We give up so much as parents and that's perfectly fine with me, I wouldn't trade it for the world! But our bed, well our room, is really the last little thing that is OURS. It's our safe space. Plus, my toddler is a mover, so I never sleep when he is in our bed.

We laid a towel down and tucked him in. It wasn't even 45 seconds before he was out cold. My husband soon followed, and I laid there waiting for the silent blackness to take me to dreamland.

At 6 am, I wake up with a foot in my eyeball and the aroma of 1000 moldy Lunchables hits me like a train. The stage 2 diarrhea has begun and this isn't a drill. This also isn't a fluke. We definitely have a sick toddler. My bargaining and praying didn't work. I handle the diaper situation, and then it happened. He was wide awake for the day. Overtired, sick, and refusing to eat. It was going to be a joyous day filled with Daniel Tiger and tears. Mostly tears from me…. If we are being 100 percent honest.

Somehow we made it through the day with a few bad diapers and by the end, he ate some toast. He was ready for bed by 6 pm and I was counting my lucky stars. I ate dinner without screaming and went to bed in a silent house. Maybe my soul experience worked…

NOPE! At 10 pm the toddler wakes up with blood-shattering screams. I run in to find "Poopsplosion; the Musical." Honestly, it wasn't THAT bad, but me being the dramatic human that I am, I will tell you it was the worst. The smell was something out of a horror movie. I'll spare you the truly gory details, but it happened 4 more times, and I slept for about 2 hours on the floor while rubbing my toddlers head. It was not a pleasant night….

Yesterday was a better day. He still wouldn't eat but he was staying hydrated. By dinner time, we got him to eat 7 noodles and a Popsicle. Again, we repeat the whole mind, body, soul thing.

I just need sleep… All I want is sleep. At this point, I will take a well-seasoned nap. Bedtime comes again around 6 pm. I stand at his door and beg for sleep. "Just one night," I keep whispering while really ugly tears roll down my face. It's silent and I take every opportunity that I can to get some sleep. 10 pm rolls around and the screaming begins. I'm assuming he feels better because all he wants to do is play. All night he jumped and tossed and turned in our bed again, from 10 pm to 6 am, he was wide awake. I think we watched the same movie 3 times.... Once his heavy little eyes couldn't take it anymore, I laid him down in his room. Within seconds, he was asleep.

I got about a solid 45 minutes after he fell asleep before my body gave me the bird and woke me up. I know I have 5,000 things I need to do today, like every other Mom. So instead of starting laundry and vacuuming, I'm sitting in my empty bed writing. The cup of decaf on my nightstand is cold, and my body is exhausted.

Days like these are the things we don't talk or read about, even in the 10 self-help books you bought at Barnes and Noble when you had a mental breakdown. These are hard days/weeks/times. Having a sick kid leaves you feeling helpless and lost. You can't throw up for your kid, even though you gladly would. We handle these situations even though we have no idea how to handle them when it happens. After time, you become a pro at rolling with the punches, or the vomit or the snot. Whichever you prefer in this scenario.

These creatures are dependent on you, and you them. Isn't motherhood one giant fucked up love fest? I'll leave you with that today. Now, go wait for your kid in the pick-up line.

Little thoughts

I've said, "Please stop trying to touch the dog's butthole," way too many times for one lifetime.

You're a Mess: "Bad Moments don't Make Bad Moms"

IT'S A MAGICAL MOMENT when you find another Mom who looks like just as much of a train wreck as you do. No, I'm not talking about the cliché Movie Mom who has coffee all down the front of her and teased hair that no one would ever dare to leave the house with. I'm talking about real Moms. The Mom who is very clearly wearing the same yoga pants as yesterday, and she's totally ROCKING them. I see you, girl. I see that yogurt stain, and I'll match that yogurt stain with a peanut butter stain.

You can always tell the Cool Moms from the normal Moms. It's just like the cafeteria in a high school. The Cool Moms are flawless and skipping around in their pants that are clean and stuff. You try to make conversation with them, and it never works out well. They stare at you like you have a giant penis on your forehead. I run into a lot of those Moms. But the problem isn't them, it's me. I am my father's daughter and I literally know no stranger. I talk to EVERYONE. Sometimes if I have no one to talk to, I even talk to my dogs and they answer back in their own voices. Yep, I'm nuts. I know.

There was one time I met this Mom who was totally me if I was a brunette and weighed like 50 pounds less. Oh, and if I had two more kids. I won't ever forget this day because it was a bad day. My son was being a typical nightmare; screaming, biting, you know… the joys of parenthood.

We met eyes in the Target dollar section. Your kid is screaming, mine is trying to lick the cart. We both give each other the "you can handle this, you pushed a kid out of your vagina" look.

Typically, most people walk away after this point, but for some reason, I stop my cart. I look at you with your flawlessly dry shampooed ponytail and say, "We are actually having the same type of day."

For a second, you look scared and then you cry. So of course, me being an emotional basket case, I start to cry too. We stand in the dollar section and hug. Your newborn who is in your Boba is wiggling as we both cry for no reason. Or for a lot of little reasons, or maybe they were even huge reasons. Really, it's all perspective. In that moment it didn't matter, we were just two unstable humans coming together to give each other support.

After we cried and had about 40 people look at us like we were INSANE (which we were/are, because we have kids we stay at home with all day - even the store manager came over to make sure no one was dying or needed aid), we both looked at each other and said the same thing, "God, we are a mess!" We laughed, and went up and down every isle, even the ones with things we would never need.

We talked about our kids, our husbands and our clearly unstable mental states. We talked about the Mom friends we had, and the ones we didn't have. We talked about birth, child rearing, and the really gross feeling that is delivering the placenta. We bonded over the fact that motherhood isn't always glittery and fun. We talked about all the things that suck. The messy floors, the laundry room tears, the depression...

And then we laughed. These little humans come into our lives like a wrecking ball, and they change everything. Even the days that are miserable are so beautiful. Once you have kids, you really can't imagine your life being any other way. We shared so many amazing things on top of all the really shitty things. She looked at me and said, "Motherhood is like a day-old cupcake. It's kind of dry and a little gross, but you still savor every bite because it's yours."

Our life is a mess, but it's a mess I literally could NEVER trade.

At the end of our trip, we checked out and walked to the parking lot. We hugged again, exchanged numbers and parted ways. I sat in the parking lot for what felt like forever.

I texted my best friend who doesn't have kids and told her I made a Mom friend. I was so overjoyed. She was my first real Mom friend.

I didn't know the protocol for these types of things. Did you wait three days? Did I have to send a bat signal? I really wasn't sure, so I waited. Maybe she would text me first. Having social anxiety and trying to make friends is really a pain in the ass. Two days went by and I hadn't heard anything, so I shot her a text. I said, "I hope you're having a better day!"

Within a few minutes she texted me back, and we chatted about how we both didn't know if we should text first. We talked about the kids, and what we were going to attempt to get done. It was nice to connect with someone who knew exactly how I was feeling.

A few days went by and we set up a "play date." We took the little people to Target because I have a problem. We walked down isle after isle just chatting.

After another couple of weeks, we learned more about each other besides the fact that we were Moms. When it boiled down to it, the only thing we had in common was that we pushed small humans out of our crotches. There was literally nothing else to talk about, and we both knew this wasn't a friendship that would last. After a few weeks, we completely stopped talking.

I was upset and I wasn't sure why. This wasn't a life-long best friend or even a month-long best friend. I was grieving a friendship that was never there.

Being a new Mom, especially a first timer, is lonely. It's hard to describe how you can be with someone 24/7 and yet still feel so alone. My husband was back at work, and I had no adults to talk to. My only real interaction with people was in public. I was frustrated and couldn't even keep a Mom friend. I tried to talk about my frustration about being alone with a few people, and they told me, "Well, this is what happens when you have a kid."

Like it was some sort of death sentence. I had a kid, so my life and friendships were over. I didn't "need" friends because I had a kid. So, I listened to those negative comments and gave up. I was never going to have social interaction again.

For a few weeks, I did nothing but sit at home. I talked to my group of friends online, but I didn't see any adult besides my husband, who I barely got to see. This was my life, and I had to accept it - but I didn't want to.

Motherhood doesn't have to be a dark and lonely experience. I wanted to have that group of friends who had coffee and walked in the park with a full face of makeup on. While obsessing over all the people I didn't have in my life, I forgot about the ones that I did.

While I was pregnant, I joined a birth board and truly connected with a group of incredible ladies. Although they were far away, we talked as if they were right here. We spent hours in our group chat, laughing and crying together. I wasn't a failure and these were my Mom friends.

Flash forward two years, we are still connected and talk daily. These women were there for me, and vice versa. We've been through deaths, marriages, happy, and sad times together. They saved me from myself and I couldn't be more grateful for their presence in my life. I love these ladies and they put up with me.

The moral to this story is this; friends come in all shapes, sizes, and distances. Your "internet friends" are just your friends. No other description needed. When you have a genuine connection with another human being, don't downplay it because you can't see them every day.

To my ladies, thank you. Thank you for loving me, even when I was an asshole.

Little thoughts

I can always tell the state of my mental health by the length of my hair. When I'm in charge of my anxiety and depression, my hair is long. When I have no control over my mind, it's short. Mental illness is a jerk that I will never understand.

WonderMom

"Having kids makes you look stable to the people who thought you were crazy and crazy to the people who thought you were stable." – Kelly Oxford

WE LIVE in the perfect little suburban, cookie-cutter neighborhood where everyone waves to each other and all the Moms drive light colored SUVs or Minivans. I am indeed one of those as well, but not on purpose. It just happened. Our mailboxes are even in a cluster at the end of our street. Sometimes after HOA meetings, we all stand in someone's garage and drink. The ladies get some unpalatable, fancy grown up wine, and the men get their locally brewed beer. Sometimes Susie brings snicker snaps, a delightful mix of suburban hell on a plate. But don't worry, they're always organic. Gag. Our house is a cute HOA-approved beige with dark shutters and a noisy garage. It's peaceful, and sometimes entertaining. Overall, we really like it here. It's comfortable.

When living in suburbia you learn a lot about the type of person you are, or that your family is. I personally feel like I'm the white trash of the block, but only because I'm not the type of "Mom" that typically lives here. Maybe I even bring the whole neighborhood value down. Who knows.

We all know that perfect suburbia Mom. The one who was meant to be a housewife... Mine is down the block.

This is the Mom I feel like we all imagine ourselves as, well, the "before we had kids" fantasy version. She is always put-together and showered. In fact, yesterday when we talked, she had just gone to get the blowout for her perfect, long, mermaid hair. Her clothes are always ADORABLE and she wears heals everywhere. EVERYWHERE. Yesterday I saw her on a ladder changing a lightbulb in 4 inch heels. She has this tiny little laugh and just oozes perfection while I ooze sweat and probably syrup.

We had a conversation, while her kids sang the sound of music songs and mine was licking a tree, about how blessed she is. How motherhood is everything she thought it would be, and how happy she is. The inner asshole in me was like, "Bitchhhhh, you are FULL of shit." I almost laughed out loud when she said, "I don't understand how some people don't have time to do it all." Instead, I pretended that my house was clean and that there wasn't a bottle of wine on my nightstand.

Don't get me wrong, she is truly a lovely person and an excellent mother. We just aren't the same type of people.

The first time I went into her house, I was terrified to touch anything. They have two toddlers and *white* carpet. *White*.... Who the fuck has *white* carpet?

That's not even the worst of it... They have *white* couches in the "great room" and their kitchen floors are an incredible *white* barn wood tile with, you guessed it... *white* grout.

I really was super annoyed at first, even to the point of trying to catch a cleaning lady coming/leaving her house. It was a sick obsession there for a few weeks. Almost like a game every time I peeked out the window. I even spent a whole day with the blinds open and writing at the table. I saw no one, and unless she has housecleaning trolls in her basement, she's doing it all alone.

I reached a point in my judgement when I saw her walk out of her front door in an apron with a cake in her hands to greet her husband. At that moment, I looked around my house at the laundry that wasn't folded and the breakfast dishes in the sink, and laughed. I laughed until it actually hurt to breathe. Then I went and leaned over the sink and said, "Wow, I fucking suck." I said it out loud in front of my toddler and my husband. I wasn't baking pies to go with dinner, or pairing wines with our expensive braised beef. I didn't shop at Whole Foods. Eighty percent of the time I don't have pants on, let alone a coordinated outfit, and no matter how hard I try, there is always something caked on to my kid's face. This is me, and I am a domestic failure.

Now being a domestic failure is way harder than it looks. It really is hard to find other things to do besides fold laundry or make the bed every day. Dishes don't stack themselves ladies, get cracking.

I tried to "do better" as they say. I tried to keep the house spotless and have a really healthy home cooked meal every night. I tried to bake something with love every day and have myself done up to greet my husband at the door, but I realized something more valuable than perfect hair or clean pants. I am not that person, and I never will be.

This was both a teaching and a learning moment for me. We will talk about the learning moment first.

I have to accept who I am not, and so do you. I know it's so hard to not live up to your stupid expectations of yourself. As a Mom, we often set the bar unrealistically high. The worst part is, sometimes it's not even us who are setting these bars. We are surrounded by a sea of "no better, do better" Moms. These are women who live to tear down other parents for not doing what THEY think is the best.

Now don't get me wrong, I have hounded on some homies for car seat safety, but I truly don't care if you aren't into baby wearing or not. These women live to make us "lazy" Moms feel like the slime on the inside of the diaper pail bag. I spend way too much time worrying about the type of Mom I should be, not the type of Mom that I am. My son is a happy, loud little rugrat who loves. He loves everyone and everything. He gets meals that I worry about not being healthy enough at least 3 times a day, if not 50. He is loved, often bathed and in bed by 8 every night. I'm doing what I can and I'm so tired of other asshole Moms thinking that it isn't enough!

I took him to have ice cream last week and the woman in there looked at me like I was giving my child cocaine!

We have to stop caring about what other people think.

Here is what really matters in this situation, and I want you to answer these questions honestly.

1) Is your child loved? Yes/No
2) Does your child know that you love them, even if they sometimes hate you? Yes/No
3) Did you feed them today? (Rather, did you offer food? Because sometimes kids won't eat because they are jerks and like to smother their parents in worry.) Yes/No

4) Are they safe? Yes/No
5) Will they hopefully wipe your ass when you're old? Yes/No

Those are the ONLY things we should worry about. Who gives a damn if your kid is in Target with two different shoes on or has frosting everywhere. The only thing that matters is that they are loved and taken care of.

So, take a deep breath. You are doing what you can and I promise, it's good enough.

And here is the teaching moment:

After having this empowering, self-motivating, FUCK YA! speech, I decided to do what any normal human being would do. I grabbed a pack of cookies out of the pantry and headed across the street. I felt bad for all the judging I did to her truly perfect life. But that being said, I still had to find a flaw or I was going to die of a Jules-induced ulcer.

We sat out front in her wooden Adirondack chairs from Pottery Barn, and I offered her a cookie.

"No, thank you, I don't eat refined sugars," she politely said in her golden mouse voice.

We were just different people, and that was okay.

At that moment, I decided that my kind of person wouldn't bring that negativity in my life, and I knew it was time to move on. So if anyone needs me, I'll be eating Oreos on my pantry floor, pretending I have clean clothes on.

Little thoughts

Parenthood is basically the pantry scene
from Signs.

Apology Pies

MY HUSBAND is such a patient man.

I know what you're thinking, "EVERYONE says that about their husband, even though they probably want to punch him in the face."

The answer to that is yes.

But really... He is just a patient, gentle creature who deals with my crazy.

I am pretty good about admitting when I'm being crazy too. Usually well after it has all happened and I'm crying on the kitchen floor. And then when I get too crazy, I apologize, and he tells me it's nothing that he can't handle. Then I start to cry because I'm an overflowing laundry basket of emotions.

Today, I was really a special breed of crazy. Today I was an asshole, so this is me pulling on the "I was wrong" hat and writing about why my husband needs a medal, and why I need to eat an excessive amount of carbs.

We've had an insane week, more so than usual. We just moved into a really sweet cookie-cutter, Pleasantville-type neighborhood where 90 percent of the Moms drive Dodge Minivans in off-white.

I hate moving, but I had no idea how much I hated moving until I did it with a toddler. Literally, it's something that comes out of my worst nightmares. In fact, this move was so bad, I can actually think of a list of 400 things I would rather do than ever move with a toddler again. I won't give you the full list, but here are the top 3 so you get the idea.

1) Setting my hair on fire
2) Doing a kale juicing cleanse

3) Surprise/accidental butt sex.

Yeah.

On top of having a nightmare little gremlin child with my bad attitude, everything that could go wrong did. But those are tales for another day, because no one wants to hear me bitch about moving.

To add to this cluster of madness, I really don't do well with change, so moving is a really tough mental adventure for me. But also for my husband, because he has to put up with me. It's not an easy task dealing with me and our toddler, but he does it. If we are being honest, he does it so well.

Fast forward from all of this to today. I was a jerk and I know it. I was so cranky with him for not changing lightbulbs that I literally didn't say a word to him for 3 hours. OVER LIGHTBULBS. It was such a disaster, even I knew I was wrong but didn't want to admit it. When he went to do work, I sat inside, stewed in my shitty attitude like it was a bad diaper. I didn't want anyone to talk to me and tell me I was wrong, even though I knew I was...

We all get into a defensive stage when we know we've failed. It's the same type of tone that we get with our mothers-in-law when they tell us all the wrong ways we are raising our kids. The tone that can be felt, not just heard. It shatters emotional glass and wounds hearts.

That's been my tone for a few days now, and I know it has to stop. I knew a simple apology wasn't going to heal this wound. I know that my snappy tone and angry words hurt the man that I love. In an answer to my snappiness, he rightfully got snappy - which fueled my fire even more.

I said things that I didn't mean, and I let the situation around us affect - no, control - every aspect of my life. How do we move forward and away from the shitty, soul-crushing attitude?

As I stewed in my own self-pity and hate, I remembered a very important fact that is hammered into women generation after generation. "The way to a man's heart is through his stomach."

This fact is particularly true to my sasquatch-esque husband. He loves to eat and loves that I can cook. It's probably why he kept my emotionally unstable, flabby-bellied ass around in the first place. He's not much of a sweets guy, but there is one superb morsel that he likes. Lemon Meringue Pie. It can't be gross store-bought pie or have meringue made from powder. It has to be the real deal, fresh lemon juice and all.

With the words I said weighing heavy on my mind, I picked up my emotional baggage and purse (that might as well be baggage), went to the fancy health food store and picked up five Meyer lemons.

Normally, being the cheapskate that I am, I buy the 2/1 lemons that are small and hard. I knew I had messed up, so this was serious. I spent $6.32 on lemons. LEMONS for god's sake. I made sure I picked the ripest, most yellow little friends I could find. They were mocking me as I took my basket to the counter. The check-out clerk was young, and hipster-y. He asked me if I was making an environmentally-friendly lemon pledge. You really can't make this up and he was the typical sweater-clad trust fund baby, whose girlfriend was probably named Moonflower. I bet they met at Coachella. I laughed, and said, "No, I'm making my husband an apology pie."

I heard the feminist behind me scoff. I didn't have a single care to give about her judgement. I took my expensive lemons in a paper bag and left, mumbling curse words all the way to my gas-guzzling Mom mobile. I didn't belong in that stupid store, and had I just played nice, I wouldn't be in the situation I was.

I got home and started on the homemade pie crust. It's a recipe that I've used since I could Google, with a few tweaks, of course. I stood over the grater moving the frozen butter up and down, not really paying attention. I nicked my finger against the metal grater, and it hurt. "I deserved that," I mumbled to whatever higher power was listening.

The crust was resting in the fridge when I started juicing the lemons. Of course, we had just moved so I had no idea where the little juicing tool was. I used the bad end of the spoon while the lemon juice burned my finger. It took me less time to push out a baby than it did to juice these lemons. The last lemon was like the juice that never ends. It just kept coming... Pulp and seeds were in abundance. I couldn't find my strainer, so I used a flour sifter to get all the impurities out from my "labor of love" lemons.

If you've ever made a lemon meringue pie, you know that the curd is a delicate creature that requires attention to detail and mostly, love. As you pour the ingredients into a double boiler or a pot, if you know what you are doing, you have to babysit them and stir like you've never stirred before. After it gets thick and textured in all the right ways, you can set it aside. It no longer requires the babysitting and dedication to its consistency.

The pie crust went in to prebake, and then came the meringue. I love making meringue. I love how something so gross looking (egg whites) turns into this beautiful, fluffy pillow-like goodness. It's like a Cinderella transformation, but with food. I was the Fairy Godmother of egg whites, but instead of a wand, I had a KitchenAid.

Once the pie crust is baked, you fill that golden brown crust with the lemon curd. It's always a beautiful color contrast between the two. Then you delicately pillow and whip the meringue on top of the pie into soft peaks. If you're lucky, you will get the perfect meringue curl, similar to the curl on top of soft serve ice cream. It's satisfying, and frustrating all in the same little package.

After you achieve or fail at the meringue curl, you put it in the oven so that way it gets this golden brown hue. In turn, creating a crunchy yet soft topping for the decadent pie. The aroma that fills your kitchen will make it hard to focus on anything else. In that moment, there is utter bliss.

(I promise there is a point to me describing the pie like this, just hang in there.)

I pulled the pie out at the perfect moment, and there it was in all its apologetic pie glory. I stared at it and waited for my tall guy to get home. I sat at the kitchen table reflecting on how great of a wife I wanted to be. Then the epiphany hit me like a train.

Apologizing in marriage is like making a pie. The crust is the argument itself, the foundation for your frustration and anger. Then the bitter filling is where you realize that maybe you went too far. Your heart and mind are full of things that make it so you aren't quite sure how to feel. On top of all that emotion, the filling is your apology. The fluffy, yet crunchy apology. Then you get to cut the pie and consume it.

At first you don't want to do it. You want to be right and stew in your grouchiness. Then you move past it and admit defeat. You apologize and do anything to make it right.

I don't like arguing with my husband, and quite honestly, we aren't good at fighting. We don't stay mad long. Well, he doesn't. I, however, am petty and often wrong. Marriage is all about learning and loving. Every day is a different challenge. Even if everything is going wrong, there will always be magic in spending every day with your best friend. So swallow your pride and apologize.

This is for both husbands and wives, because under that layer of frustration and anger is love.

Above all else, never underestimate the power of an apology pie.

Humbled: A Weiner Story

"Having a two-year-old is like having a blender that you don't have the top for." –
Jerry Seinfeld

TODDLERS ARE the most humbling little humans. Just when you think you have a grasp on parenting them, they do something to knock your ass back down to reality. They know when we think we're in charge and they remind you that you're merely a peasant in their world, only in charge of getting fruit snacks.

Last week we experienced one of those moments. We stopped in at Walgreens to pick up some things and let Tater use the potty. It was just me and the two boys in line. I had the baby carrier in one hand, and our items and my wallet in the other. Tater was standing by my side in the long line. He was spinning around and looking at candy. I kept asking him to just stand still, be patient, wait just a little longer. He wasn't having it, like most 3-year-old kids. He finally came and stood in front of me, swinging his arms around. I looked down at Tot to make sure he was doing okay. All of a sudden, I feel something hit my foot. I look up and it's Tater's pants.

What happened next was basically in slow motion.

He looked around, shook his hips and shouted, "LOOK AT MY WIENER!"

I froze for half a second before throwing my items to the ground. With one hand I attempted to pull his pants up from around his ankles. He giggled and tried to run away saying, "You can't catch me!" I one-handedly wrestled his shorts on, breaking a minor sweat in the process. For some reason, I didn't think of setting the baby seat down.

Tater was still laughing as I looked up to see what kind of judgment I was getting. The two men in the line in front of me were laughing. One (who probably had kids and had been there) had tears in his eyes. The woman at the front of the line just glared at me like it was my fault that my kid thinks his penis is hilarious. I did the shameful head nod while making a face of apology, mixed with Chrissy Teigen's legendary Golden Globe's face.

I tried to use this as a teaching moment. I (tried to) calmly explain that we don't pull our pants down in public. He didn't give two shits. He had an audience laughing at him. He knew he did something I didn't like, which, in his mind was pure gold. He made this cheesy ass face at me. I tried not to smile. I was so embarrassed, yet not embarrassed enough to leave.

Without really thinking about what I was saying, I said, "Buddy, you can't do that when you're 18. They'll make you register as a sex offender."

At this point, the bearded gentleman in front of me absolutely lost it. He laughed a deep, belly laugh. I nervous giggled, because that had just come out like stressful word vomit. I need to find a new coping mechanism other than dry humor and sarcasm.

The line moved quickly at that point and we got out of there. I was knocked off my parenting pedestal.

I called the Sasquatch when I got to the car. We laughed... oh boy, did we laugh. This kid throws us for a loop every day. Some days we have minimal control, other days we have absolutely none. We are learning, every day.

Cravings

CRAVINGS ARE THE STRANGEST part of life. They come with such force and intensity. They know exactly what they want.... They make your brain itch, twitch, and salivate until you get that craving into your body. Sometimes we have these cravings because we are missing something from our diet. Other times, it's a mind/matter thing... We cave, or we fight off the cravings with something "good enough." It's a human nature thing, not just a pregnancy thing.

Food cravings are easy to satisfy. As a pregnant woman, I appreciated the donut holes that I was craving even if they didn't align with my diet plan. When I first got pregnant with Tater, I knew I would have them. I waited for my first craving to come. When it did, the craving was gas station taquitos of all things. Then my cravings evolved into things I was less ashamed to eat.

As my pregnancy came to an end, I figured the cravings would go away. Once again, they evolved. When you're a parent, you crave new things... Things that can't be bought in a gas station at 3 am. You crave alone time, adult interaction, the option for a scolding hot meal, and my personal favorite; silence.

Tonight, I am craving total and utter silence. Usually when I have this craving for the absence of noise, quiet will do. Not tonight. I need the void of all sound. It's been a week, to say the least. Between all of us battling the flu, Sasquatch staying home, the coughing, sneezing, barfing, dog howling, and the constant hum of a humidifier, I am done with noise. Even the sound of my own nasally breathing was beginning to annoy me. This bone-deep craving was one that my mental health couldn't afford to ignore.

I listened to my soul telling me to cut the noise. I made my bed and began to turn down the volume. My phone went silent and my watch off. All the TVs in the house were dark and the video monitor was muted. I sat on my bed waiting.

There was still noise. The gentle whistle of the wind blew through the narrow strip in between our suburban homes. The crisp smell of fall seeped through the window. The ceiling fan whirled above me, motor softly humming. The light bulb next to me somehow managing to buzz. I said "no."

I closed the window tightly, shut off my ceiling fan, and turned out my lamp. I closed my eyes and listened. There. Was. Still. Noise. Why?

I listened closely for what, exactly, was making the last tiny but of sound.

Did my dog always breathe so obnoxiously? I kicked him out of my bedroom. "Sorry dog, you have to go right now." He looked at me with his sad, brown eyes as I closed the door in his face. My bed called me back. Again, I listened.

The candle I had lit was making the slightest flickering noise. Not today, candle. I blew it out with one hasty, slightly annoyed breath and waited. I waited for the next minuscule noise to disturb my craving.

There was only silence.

I seized my opportunity and closed my eyes. The blanket of silence laid on my shoulders like a warm hug. The pure satisfaction of fulfilling a craving swept me from my feet and carried me in its gentle arms. This was better than any donut hole or corn dog nugget.

Simon and Garfunkel were right; there is a sound of silence, and tonight that was the sound of pure bliss. I stayed stationary for 15 minutes. I focused on the absence of noise. I listened to my breathing, as nasally as it is. I heard the light crinkle my pants made when shifting. I heard nothing more than the sound of my own mind shutting off just for a few minutes. No timers, cries, nose blows, or dog chirps.

The silence was like my own mental health tech support - turning the power off and then back on again. Instead of them resetting my network connectivity, it reset my patience, spirit, and joy.

My life is noisy and pure chaos. It's crammed with busy schedules, silly songs, sticky fingers, and full hearts. My 15 minutes of soul resetting silence was everything I needed. It reminded me of all the things I love in this household, and mess. I love the laughter, the love, and even the damn dog with the annoying breathing. I needed my reset.

I know you've read me mumble on about self-care, but dear god, it's so important. Even just my 15 minutes of silence, followed by 30 minutes of writing (so only keys clicking) really fixed my exhausted spirit. I feel like tonight, I can actually rest, and not just have my eyes closed for a few hours.

As I come back to my noise filled reality, I will hold on to the sound of silence. Indulge in your mental health cravings, friends. It's worth it.

10 things no one told me about having kids

1. When you sneeze while breastfeeding, you can experience a let-down.
2. Sleeping when the baby sleeps is unrealistic and hearing that phrase will make your eye twitch.
3. Little boys get erections and when you call your husband freaking out about it, he will laugh at you.
4. You will catch an unholy amount of vomit in your hands, hair, and cleavage - or the H.H.C. if you will.
5. When you potty train your kid, you still have to wipe their ass for a while. That doesn't just end.
6. You will end up wanting a Minivan, even if you repress the feelings.

7.   The amount of guilt you will feel
       about every decision you make
       will weigh heavy on you, even
       when those around you validate
       your choices.

8.   You might not connect with your
       baby right away, and that's okay.

9.   YOU HAVE TO DELIVER THE
       PLACENTA.

10.   Did I mention the ass wiping
       thing? Because that one shocked
       me to my core.

Modern Feminism and its Failure to Stay-at-Home Moms

I DON'T GET POLITICAL OFTEN, and when I do, I try really hard not to offend others. Today I'm getting political. I want to talk about modern feminists and being a stay-at-home Mom.

I am all for true feminism, which is defined as: the advocacy of women's rights on the basis of the equality of the sexes. I believe that all women should be equal in every way, but for some reason, modern feminists aren't searching for equality but superiority. This is NOT all feminists; just a select bunch who are willing to burn down men and any women who don't agree with them. They are not true feminists.

I am a stay-at-home Mom, a wife, and partner in my marriage. We do statically gender role things in our marriage and I am sick of being belittled for it.

Yep, I do the laundry, dishes, and keep the house clean. I do the shopping, cooking, and "child rearing" solo for 10-hours a day, four days a week. My husband is the sole provider for our household. He makes the money, I just spend it at Target. The way we run our household works for us. I know my husband is more than capable of doing these things, but this is how I contribute.

I've learned that I shouldn't tell people without kids (especially women) that I am a stay-at-home Mom. If I do tell people, it sometimes comes with acceptance or this complete look of betrayal. I've had someone say to me:

"Do you realize how far you are setting back women?"

"I'm sad you are wasting your worth/education/dreams."

"That's really disappointing."

"You're worth so much more than that. Your husband should value that."

"You could go back to work. Unless your husband won't let you."

"You're failing every woman who has ever worked for equality."

This isn't even all the things that I've heard about being a stay at home parent. This isn't even the worst of them! These are things that have been said straight to my face. The things that have been said over the internet are far worse.

There are so many misconceptions that come with being a stay-at-home parent, and a lot of them revolve around feminism or what people think is feminism. I want to clear these up because I am damn tired of being told I'm less of a woman for staying home with my child.

1. No one forced me to be married. My Dad didn't trade my "hand" for a prized freakin' heifer. (Although, there was this one

time in South Dakota at a gas station by the Corn Palace when a stranger offered a pig for me. He might have considered it, I'm not sure.) I'm really happy to be married to a man who lifts me up every day.

2. No one forced me to have babies. I am not a machine for producing children. Now, was my delicate bundle of sass a surprise? Yes, he was. BUT NO ONE FORCED ME TO HAVE A CHILD.

3. I was not forced to quit my job or leave my dreams behind. If anything, having a child and staying home has pushed me closer to my dream of being a published author. I have to go about things differently, but my drive to succeed is no different than it was. I have goals, I will meet those goals, and I will do it while raising a small human.

4. I AM NOT SETTING WOMEN'S RIGHTS BACK BY BEING A MOM, WIFE, OR STAY-AT-HOME PARENT. Being a Mom is so empowering for me. My body made a person, and then I shoved another person out. Of course, I am going to want to be with this person! Yes, I do miss working sometimes. There are days where I question every life choice I've ever made, but I LOVE what I do! Why isn't that enough for some people?

Feminism should be about equality and empowering women. If no one is getting hurt or being forced into a life they don't want, then why are we degrading others?

Why does it matter if I make my husband pies and raise my baby from home? I admire working parents so much, so why do they belittle those who stay home? Why do we assume that women are forced into these things? Why do you assume that our husbands don't value us? WHY? So many questions and I never seem to get an answer other than, "Well, you should know what you are doing wrong."

So "modern feminism," you have absolutely failed the stay-at-home parent. Let's fix that. To all my true feminists, you keep on doing your thing. No matter what you do, you are valued.

The Storm During the Calm

THERE IS AN ASPECT to my motherhood journey that has changed who I am.

I suffered from postpartum mood disorders twice. With my first son, Tater, I had a traumatic delivery that resulted in a NICU stay. Our first stay lasted 9 grueling and unexpected days. We went into delivery thinking we'd be delivering a perfectly healthy baby. It crushed me and made me feel like a complete failure. I couldn't hold my baby for 3 days. I had to stare at him just lying there, connected to all sorts of wires, monitors, and needles.

I stayed strong, but my god, was I sad. "Any new Mom with a NICU baby is going to be sad," is what I told myself. This was more than just sadness - deep down I knew that. I shoved it deep into a box in the bottom of my soul. Then a weight was lifted. We were going home in the middle of a snow storm. We were leaving the safety net of the hospital for the first time, driving 45 minutes home with a baby that I just had pushed out of my body 9 days prior.

"How do they just let people leave with these things?" I thought. The anxiety the entire ride home was the worst anxiety of my life.

We made it home with a healthy baby and I could breathe again. I still wasn't myself, but I figured that was just parenthood.

That is NOT parenthood.

The next week, I literally don't remember... I just remember little blurbs.

One night, I noticed that our little guy was sniffling and I panicked. The nurse's line said it was likely a cold and to just monitor him... I had this irrational fear that it was RSV. He started wheezing and I ran to Children's Hospital. We waited in the lobby with a sick infant for

2 hours, and then a room for another hour and a half. When the doctor came in, I expressed my concerns. I begged for them to do an RSV test and he said, "It sounds like acid reflux," and sent us home… My instincts were screaming at me, but who was I, a first time Mom to tell a doctor he was wrong?

We went back to the ER at 5 am that night for the same encounter. I begged and begged. "Reflux," a doctor said. I called his pediatrician the second they opened and away we went. I explained the symptoms to her and she tested him for RSV. It was instantly positive. The pediatrician said we had to go to the hospital again… We drove another 45 minutes to the hospital and rechecked in. My husband and I were both getting sick and the NICU asked us to stay away if we had a fever. We left our baby there again… and drove home.

I broke down. The tears, the panic…. all of it hit me like a train. I gathered all the clothes, sheets and towels from the house and went to the laundromat at 10 pm. I disinfected every square inch of the house. I sobbed over a Lysol-soaked towel until the first light of the day. I laid in bed for 3 days after that. The first day was due to a fever, the two days after that were because I literally just couldn't bring myself to move.

My best friend forced me to go out to lunch with her and she told me that I needed help. She wasn't wrong... I called my doctor from the parking lot and said I thought there was something wrong. I said that I just couldn't feel normal, and he cut me off.

"I'll prescribe Celexa. Ask the pharmacist if you have questions." He hung up. I felt better about getting help, yet I didn't know what was wrong or what my options were.

The medication helped, but I was still wrapped up in the stigma of mental health care. At my 6-week appointment, I was officially diagnosed with postpartum depression.

I knew that I had it, but hearing it from a doctor in-person really set it in stone... I struggled with coming to terms with my mental illness. I took my antidepressant consistently for 3 months. I was feeling normal, so I thought it was time to stop taking my medication... by myself... without doctor approval....

Yeah, not my brightest moment.

During all of this, we got hit with THOUSANDS of dollars in NICU bills because of an error from the insurance company. Our finances were tight which added more stress and my husband started working nights. I went back to work to try and help with our expenses, but we were drowning in every aspect. Mentally, physically, and financially, we were drowning.

One day after work, I got in my car and just started driving. My family didn't need me. I was a bad Mom, a bad wife, and a failure. I was just going to run away. I got almost to the border of another state. I came to my senses and realized my postpartum depression wasn't gone, and I needed help.

I got home and hugged my baby. I was so lucky that I realized I wasn't okay. I called my doctor and did research again. That's when I found my people. I found a non-profit that dedicated its whole existence to educating, helping and loving those struggling with a postpartum mood disorder.

I let that swallow me. I was going to help others get through this, and it was going to heal me. In many ways, it did. I still had bad weeks... I still struggled with myself and my mind. I loved helping others feel safe, validated and needed. This was my place.

The knowledge, friendship and strength these other Moms gave me, saved my life. They made it so that I didn't fear having another baby or getting PPD again. I knew I could save so many Moms who were in my shoes because of the tools that were given to me. The stigma surrounding mental illness for me was stomped so deep into the ground. I was a warrior.

Then baby #2, Tot, was born. I felt great! They let me take this baby home within 26 hours of delivering him. Seriously, they really let you leave with fresh babies - it blew my mind. He was the easiest baby, and things were great! I thought I had escaped mental illness.

Then the anxiety hit me, and it hit HARD. I wasn't depressed or sad... but I was really anxious. I knew exactly what to do and had no shame doing it. I called my doctor and we had a long soul-healing chat. This doctor seriously erased all the trauma that my first delivery and old doctor had created. We decided an anti-anxiety medication along with a therapist were the best possible options. I love my therapist, so I had no issues seeing her and opening up.

The knowledge that I had gained saved me this time. I'm not afraid, I am a warrior.

If you or anyone you know is struggling with mental illness, reach out. There is help available and it does get better.

A Haiku

Why don't my kids sleep?
I just want to be rested
Send Starbucks gift cards.

Toddlers. Am I right?

"Even freshly washed and relieved of all obvious confections, children tend to be sticky." — Fran Lebowitz

WHEN WE START to get more comfortable with parenthood, we get a little cocky. "We've got this, we can handle anything!" We've all been there...
WRONG.

Just when I think I have a firm grasp on the balls that are parenthood, I am pushed off my pearly white pedestal with a crisp slap of reality. Here is that reality today.

I have no clue how to parent my toddler.

There it is in large, bold text. I even centered it, so you know this is serious. 12-point font, really, just wasn't getting the point across.

I've spent the better part of the last 6 months trying to find my role. I've read the parenting books (that I typically don't like) from all ends of the spectrum. I've read the crunchy Mom guidelines about being a parent that blow positivity and glitter out of their dirt star, to the books that say everything I'm feeling.

For example, "Like serial killers, toddlers lack empathy." ("Toddlers Are Assholes and It's Not Your Fault" by the HILARIOUSLY brilliant, Bumni Laditian. Read it.)

These books are all so great. Really, they are! They help so many people. Yet here I sit, on my bed, surrounded by laundry and broken dreams, still not knowing what the fuck I'm doing.

Every. Single. Day is something different. Just when I think my book is full of tricks, I realize that I truly know nothing, and my toddler is outsmarting me. He knows he's smarter than I am, too.

Just the other day I told him to do something. He shot back the cheesiest, evilest little grin while replying with a firm, "No thanks." At least he's polite? I often find myself staring into his beautiful blue eyeballs, wondering how such a tiny human can be so amazing and terrifying all at once.

I know I'm not alone in feeling this way because I see the same "type" of Mom standing next to me in the "Parenting Help" section looking confused, tired, and mentally over it. The books fly off the shelves, and Mom blogs are more popular than ever.

The other day, I sat with two books on my nightstand that totally contradicted one another, leaving me more lost than when I started. I took to the online forums, which was a huge mistake because "Sancti-Mommies" flock like seagulls to a French fry when you ask about discipline.

Squaaaack know better, do better squaaaaaack

Did I mention I hate Sancti-Mommies? I tried taking a little bit of advice from everything I read. So far, some things are working, some aren't. I'm still on the verge of insanity but I'm learning that it's okay to have no clue what you are doing.

What it boils down to is this simple message - no one has any idea what the fuck they are doing. They can pretend all they want. The harsh reality is kids are insane, but we love them. We are never going to know exactly what to do for every single kid, because like pimples, all kids are different. Go with the flow, learn as you go, and make sure there is one place in your house where you can lock yourself in for 38 seconds of sanity.

I think of it this way; these kids have lived longer than all of my house plants. Can I get an Amen?

No.

ONE OF THE BIGGEST lessons I've learned as a Mom is that it's okay to say "no." Not only is saying "no" to your kid 80 percent of your daily vocabulary, but it's okay to say "no" to other people. You don't owe anyone anything.

This is something I struggled with for a really long time. I felt that I owed everyone my time, energy, attention, money and time with my kids. I'm not telling you to be an asshole and not do kind things for others, but if doing something for someone else leaves you empty instead of fulfilled, say "no."

You aren't required to go to birthday parties or bring your kids to places. You don't have to let people hold your freshly-born baby. You don't have to host Thanksgiving if you don't want to.

The only obligation you have as a Mom is to make sure you and your kids are okay.

Practice it. Say "no" right now.

No.

NO.

No, thanks.

Fuck no.

No, that's okay.

No, we're fine.

No, not today.

There are all sorts of ways to say no. Say it fearlessly and kindly. You don't owe anyone a thing.

Failure

"The quickest way for a parent to get a child's attention is to sit down and look comfortable." — Lane Olinghouse

FAILURE. It's a small word that when used properly, packs the punch of a thousand fists. It's almost as bad as when you were a kid and your parents used, "I'm not mad, just disappointed."

Being a parent (and as a new parent, I feel it a lot) is often feeling like you could/should have done things better or differently.

"We should have saved better."

"We should have planned better."

"We should have made sure things were taken care of."

These are just a few of the things my sweet husband and I have tossed around in the past few weeks - months actually. Then when the "should have/ could haves" start to pile up and there becomes more every day, you get lost in it. It's like the mind is drowning in a constant reminder that you have done something wrong... or to easily put it, you've failed.

I constantly feel like I'm failing everyone around me. My friends, my family, my son - but who I really feel like I've failed is myself. Once you are in this "shoulda/coulda/woulda" mindset, it seems so easy to find everything you hate about yourself and about your life. I knit-pick at my body because I've failed to lose the baby weight. I knit-pick our finances because I shouldn't have quit my job. I start seeing everything I do as a complete failure. Then things start actually going wrong. I will burn dinner or shrink my shirt. Then a small, but intense meltdown happens...

I start babbling about how I'm a failure, I'm in debt to my eyeballs, I'm not doing what I wanted to. I've never been traveling or this, that and the other thing. Sometimes, depending on what is going wrong, I say that I shouldn't be a Mom and that I've failed at being able to take care of my son. It turns in to a high school fight with a mean girl, but that mean girl is myself.

Something magical happens at that point. My sweet, patient Husband usually wraps me in a hug and reminds me of all the wonderful things in our life together. Usually, it takes me a few minutes to let it sink in.

However, living is expensive, so my 'Squatch has to work. Sometimes I naturally feel this way when he's gone. I break down and do the whole process all over again. Sometimes I use my feelings of total failure to clean my house. I harness the evil for good, I suppose. I can't always aggressively Swiffer, so when that doesn't work, my mind runs wild. I argue with myself about how we will fix the scary things in our life and how I will lose the weight. I worry about what dinner will be and when the couch will get vacuumed.

Last night was one of those nights. I was worried, scared and felt like I had truly failed. My group of Mom friends had a rough day and we took it out on one another. I feel like I failed as a friend. Tater wouldn't stop crying and I didn't know why... another feeling of failure, and to top it all off, I forgot to cook dinner for 'Squatch who was at work all day. That's three "failures" on top of the others that loom over me.

I cried.

(I firmly believe that the universe is an amazing place, in which everything happens for a reason.)

As I was sobbing, I opened Facebook, and the first post I see is from my friend's mother: "I haven't failed, I've just found 10,000 ways that don't work."

I opened my crusty, teary eyes and laughed.

It's amazing how some things just punch you in the face when you need it the most. I haven't failed as a Mom, I have just found some ways not to be the Mom I want to be. I'm not failing at losing the 'baby weight', I've just learned there are 10,000 snacks you shouldn't eat. I didn't fail as a friend or a wife.

What's amazing is that I can still make mistakes, but I'm not failing. So now that I've found the ways that don't work, it's time to start appreciating the things that do work. I have to embrace the things that I suck at and try to make them better.

So here is to you, and all that ways that you're going to find that don't work. Eventually, you will find a way that does.

3+1=Fuck

"You can learn many things from children. Like how much patience you have, for instance." — Franklin Jones

TODDLERS ARE the world's best birth control.

I say that affectionately. Everything is loud, sticky, and so beyond frustrating. I feel like they should train S.W.A.T. negotiators by having them try to put toddlers to bed or feed them any sort of food that isn't a fruit snack. I love my son, but holy mother of god, is he a lot to handle (and that's okay).

When we found out that we were indeed expecting baby #2, I was elated... after about a week of sheer panic, wondering how the fuck I'm going to handle a new baby and a Tater.

Tater was 2.5 years old when we found out about our newest root vegetable. He was in full swing of the terrible twos. He is the most wild, free-spirited, mildly feral little boy I've ever met. He does have a heart of pure gold, but he never stops moving. There were days when the fire station sounded like a really great option to leave myself. It's a safe space, right?

The idea that I could potentially have two mini-dictators running through my house without pants on TERRIFIED ME. I hoped and hoped for a mellow girl, but that just wasn't in the cards for us.

We found out Tot was a boy, and I experienced some gender disappointment. I was so happy he was healthy, but man… I wanted a girl. In my mind, a girl would be easier and was less likely to flash her parts in public. A girl would be mellow and kind. Another boy would be pure chaos. I had a good ugly cry over the fact that it was a boy. Then my sweet, wild boy came up, gave me a kiss and said, "Love you Mama! You're beautiful!"

Little boys may be wild and rowdy, but man do they love their Mamas. I was so lucky (and scared) to have two little boys. I could handle anything that was thrown my way and so can you.

Adding another boy to our house basically turned this place into a Paw Patrol-themed frat party. Someone is always naked, something is always sticky, and there are cups EVERYWHERE.

Someone is always screaming or farting. Seriously, having little boys is basically just one continuous fart sound.

I say, "Stop playing with your wiener," way more than I would like. I can only imagine what this house will become when Tot starts talking.

Having two kids is terrifying, but so worth it.

Plus, if one kid doesn't want to take care of me when I'm old, at least I have hope in the other one.

#Blessed

"Being a mother is learning strengths you didn't know you had and dealing with fears you didn't know existed." — Linda Wooten

I DON'T LIKE being a Mom today. My cup isn't "running over," it's actually bone dry. I don't feel #blessed. More like #deaddogtired.

I'm feeling overwhelmed, overtired and under-appreciated. My well of patience is currently in a drought. I'm stuck at the pool because I'd rather be in public losing my shit. It's hot. Tater isn't listening, and I'm just over it.

Before you think, "Well, maybe you shouldn't have had kids," or other nonsense, let me explain. I love my children. I love being a Mom and I truly am grateful for the life I live.... but being grateful and being a little over it are two separate things.

Parenthood is a job that you don't get a break from. You can't just clock out at 5 and be done. The only payment you get is boogers handed to you and rock-hard chicken nugget treasures you find when you finally find the time to clean your car.

Like everything in life, we get burnt out. We forget about self-care and prioritizing what is actually important and what seems important. It's a balance that some days I master and others, I fail.

Tonight, after I struggle with the typical bed time routine, I'm shutting down for a bit. Like the battery on our forever draining phones, *we* need to charge, too. Whether it's a bath, a book, or maybe breaking a plate... we all need self-care.

Today, I don't like being a Mom and that's okay.

Take care of yourselves.

Things I've Googled During My Time as a Mom

1. What color is baby poop supposed to be?
2. Removing feces from cashmere
3. Removing poop stains from couch
4. How to get a Hot Wheel out of a toilet that's been flushed
5. How old is the maximum age to leave kids at the fire station?
6. Coffee delivery near me
7. Why don't my kids fucking sleep?
8. At what age do kids wipe their own ass?
9. How do you teach a kid to wipe his own ass?
10. Minivans for sale near me
11. How to get the Paw Patrol theme song out of your head
12. Toddler boarding schools
13. Is my toddler a sociopath?

14. Why is my baby so sweaty all the
     time?
15. Symptoms of (insert every illogical
     illness here)
16. Is Desitin toxic to dogs?

Today Didn't Suck

"One thing about having children is that even as it complicates many aspects of your life, it simplifies others." — Katie Kitamura

EVERY INSTAGRAM MOM on planet Earth (including me) is always like, "Oh, we don't talk about the bad days!" Then proceed to make a long-winded post underneath a black and white photo about the bad days of motherhood.

It's all an attempt to normalize real motherhood, which I freakin' love. I love that we all want to be more real and genuine with each other. However, with posting all of our bad days (with good intentions), we've lost sight that there are some really beautiful days of motherhood.

I had a really fantastic day with my kids. They have both been functioning members of society... well, as "functioning" as a 3-year-old and 4-month-old can be. There was only one minor meltdown for both children. This is unheard of for any household. No one ran outside naked or tried to ride the dog. It was basically Christmas.

We laughed today, a lot. 3-year-olds are really hilarious in their own weird way. We successfully did some craft that I was really bad at. I answered all of my 3-year-old's questions without losing my effin' mind. Tot didn't have an emotional breakdown or shit up his back. I didn't feel overwhelmed, under-appreciated or excessively sweaty. There were no unusual bodily fluids on any of my apparel. I was patient, understanding and didn't worry about the housework. Bedtime was literally a slice of fucking pie. Tater crawled into his bed and said he loved me. Tot went down without turning into a pterodactyl.

It was a damn good day, and I'm going to cherish the hell out of it.

The good days may be few and far between with young children, but they are there. They deserve to be celebrated and talked about just as much as the bad days. The balance between the good and bad days is real motherhood. Not every day is cupcakes and unicorn farts, but not every day sucks either.

Embrace it.

So Wrong That You're Still Wrong

"Admitting that you fucked up and making light of it and being okay with it and wanting to learn more is the most powerful fucking thing you can do as a human being. It's the only thing you're supposed to be doing. It's the way we make connections as a human being." — Karen Kilgariff and Georgia Hardstark

YOU'RE GOING TO FEEL like a failure. You're going to make mistakes. You're going to be wrong.

These three things are so hard to accept as a parent. It's almost as if we forget that we are human beings. We know our kids are going to make mistakes, but we don't expect the mistakes made by us. We don't want to be wrong. We are the parents and should always be right, right? Wrong.

I personally have unrealistic expectations of myself, always. It's one of my biggest downfalls. I feel that nothing I do is ever good enough. I fear making mistakes in my parenting choices. I fear doing something wrong and it effecting the kids.

It's time to set the unrealistic expectations aside and just be okay with being human. We can't just be right because we are the parents. There are two ways you can handle being wrong. You can brush it off and pretend that you're always right. Inevitably, showing your kids that parents don't make mistakes and setting them up for failure as a future parent. Or you can admit that you're wrong. Show that everyone does things they shouldn't have done or said things they don't mean. It takes a lot of courage, but it's something we have to do.

There's going to be a day where you have to look your child in the eyes and admit that you were wrong. Today was that day for me.

I lost my absolute shit with Tater. My patience disappeared, and I yelled. I yelled about something that didn't matter, which really broke my little guy's spirit. I said "salty words" like "fuck," "goddamn," and "son of a bitch." We both started to cry on the floor of my living room. The tears were ugly. He apologized, which made me feel even worse. It wasn't his fault that I fucking lost it. It wasn't his fault that I was tired and being an asshole because of the things I can't control. It's not his fault that I gave him playdoh that logically I knew would get stuck in our brand new carpet.

I looked him in his little blue eyes and told him to not apologize. I said, "Mama is so sorry she yelled at you. I was wrong, and I'm sorry."

Swallowing the pride it took to do that was hard. My internal dialogue was telling me that, *"I'm not allowed to do this. I'm not allowed to be wrong."*

Which has a lot to do with the cycle I was raised with. (See — this all connects!)

He looked at me through the thick eyelashes that boys have but don't deserve and said, "It's okay, Mama! I not mad!"

He was back to being happy and lovely, but I still felt like a bag of dicks.

This isn't going to be the only time that I'm wrong and have to admit it. Shit, I'm basically a professional at being wrong. As a parent, you should get real used to being wrong. Own it and shout it from the rooftops. "Today, I was wrong, and I wasn't an asshole because I admitted to my kids that I was wrong."

That might be my life motto from this point forward.

The Fire Station is Free

"If evolution works, how come mothers only have two hands?" – Nia Vardalos

THIS STORY IS PROOF that even perfect mothers, like myself, do stupid things. Back when I only had one crotch fruit to look after, I went to Target (shocking, I know). Tater was about 6-months-old and still in the infant car seat. When we left the store, I did my usual routine. Stuff loaded in the trunk and then the baby in the car. As I was loading the baby into his car seat, I somehow locked the doors. For some odd reason, I put my purse in the front seat, which I never do. I closed the door and walked around to the driver's side. Locked... Fuck. I tried all 4 doors, they were locked.

I immediately panicked and hollered at the first person I could see. Thank goodness, this woman didn't flinch when an overweight, under-showered manic ran toward her in the parking lot. I told her what was happening and she let me use a phone to call a locksmith. It would take them 30-plus minutes to get to me.

The wonderful woman who came to my rescue advised that I call the fire department. Within minutes, two huge fire trucks pull in with the lights and sirens blaring loud for all to hear. They drew the eyes of every single person in the parking lot. Luckily, it was Target on a Friday morning, so 99 percent of the parking lot were other Moms. They all watched as three super kind (and pretty attractive) firemen unlocked my car for me. Some had looks of sympathy on their faces, others were with judgement.

Multiple people came over to tell me that it was okay and that it happens to the best of us. All while I was sobbing in the ugliest manner possible. I'm pretty sure I had a snot bubble at one point. It only took the firemen about 4 minutes to break into my car. They explained to me that this happens once a day, every day.

I was thankful for the kindness I received from so many strangers, and I was also thankful that it was cold outside.

When the car was unlocked, I scooped up my baby who was laughing hysterically. He thought this was the greatest thing ever. Isn't it fitting that this kid laughed at the fact that I was completely mortified?

The fire department is way faster than a locksmith, so there's a good resource for you.

Live. Laugh. Learn. Keep parenting on, you lovely humans.

CPSIA information can be obtained
at www.ICGtesting.com
Printed in the USA
LVHW051816191118
597624LV00007B/535